~Introduction~

While attending a Japanese public school, Japanese was NOT one of my best subjects. I struggled with writing Chinese characters, or kanji. The amount required for school overwhelmed me and the repetitive practices bored me. Now I want to reverse all that by sharing with you in my colouring-in creation journey.

The first step, "Colouring Enoughness", was about recovering my passion for art, which had been all but crushed by postnatal depression. "I am enough" helped in many aspects of my life. "I am enough to have and enjoy a fulfilling relationship." "I am enough to enjoy playfulness every day." Repeating such statements gradually restored my self-esteem and creativity.

"I am enough to be at peace."

Then I thought that perhaps "I am enough to be at peace with Japanese". At the core, kanji characters are symbols, just shapes. What if I got back to basics and simply appreciated their visual beauty? Why have the pressure of stroke correctness and order, and the dullness of repeating 10 times to get it just right? Why not take an entirely visual approach, like a designer or decorator?

So here is another step in the colouring-in journey, with elegant, beautiful and novel shapes for you to enjoy.

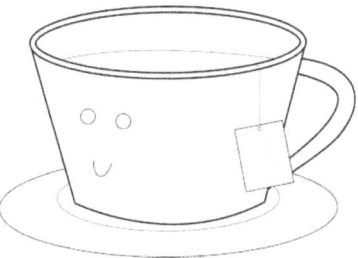

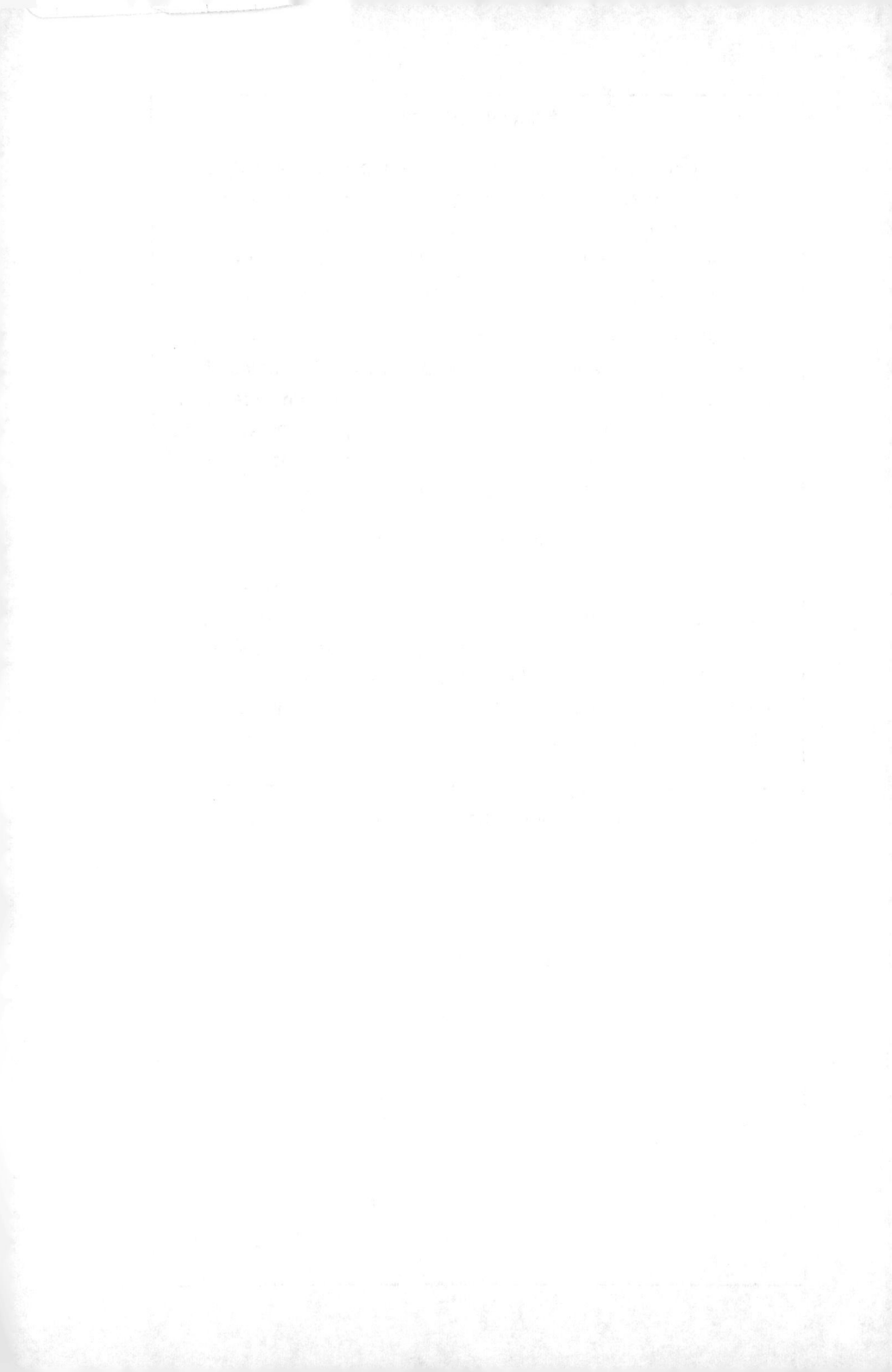

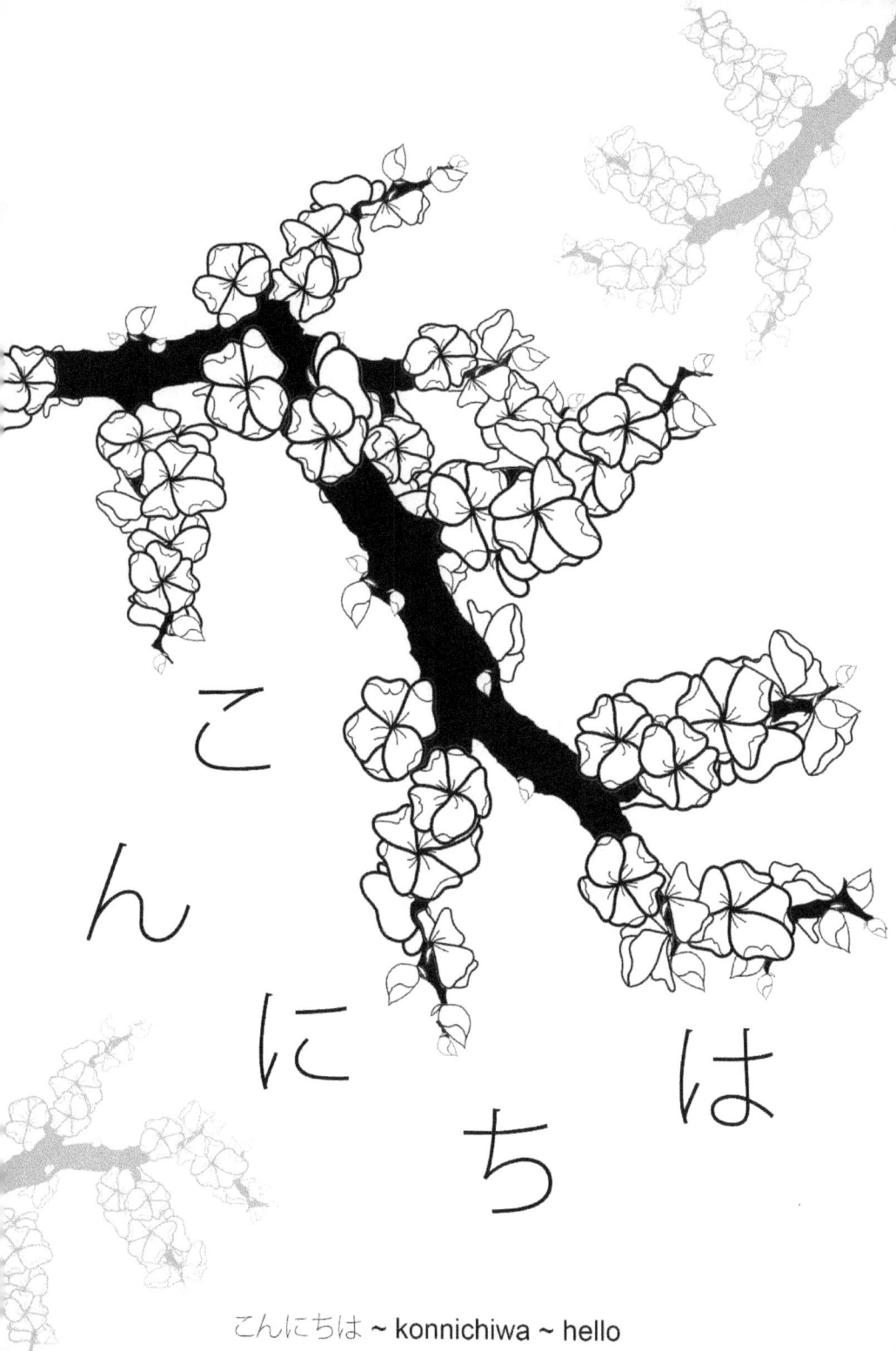

こんにちは ~ konnichiwa ~ hello

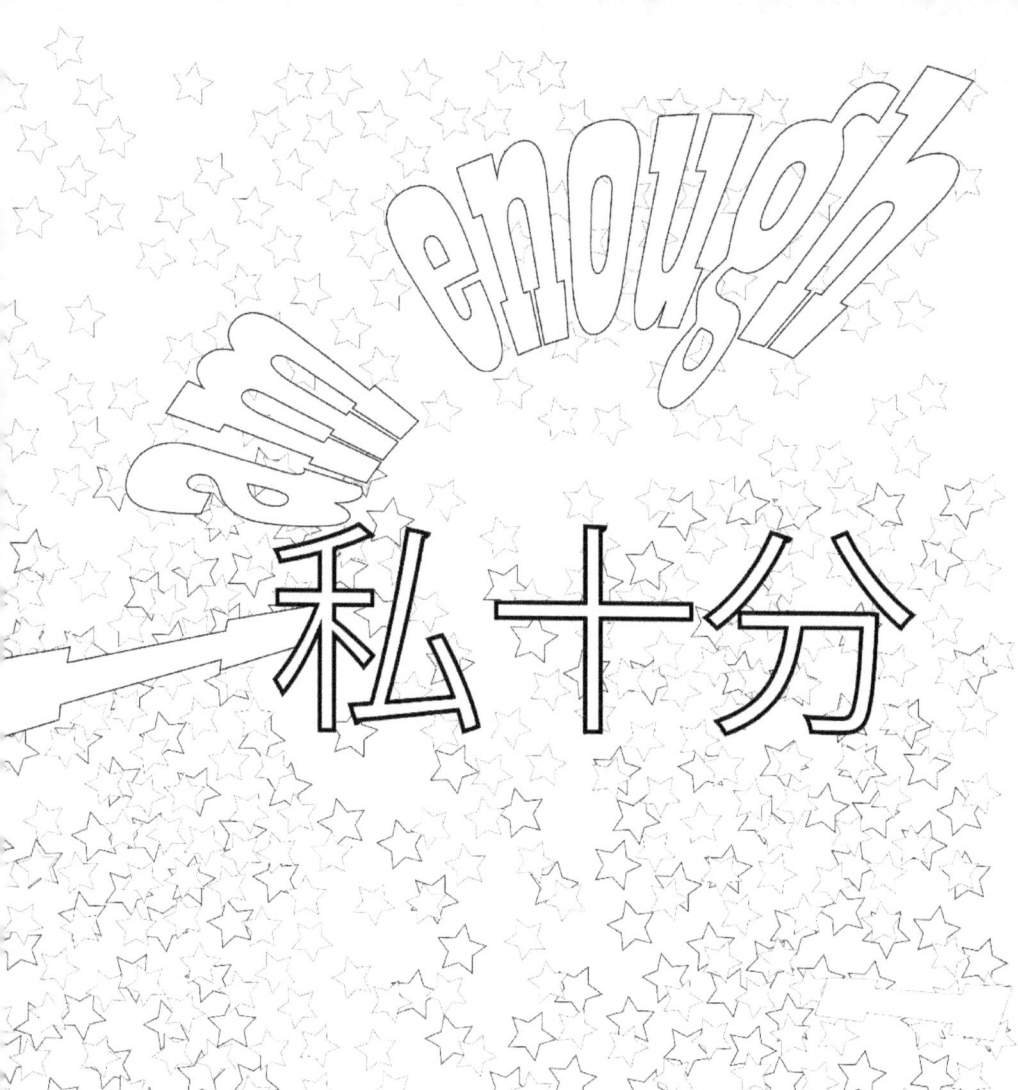

私十分 ~ watashi juubunn ~ I am enough

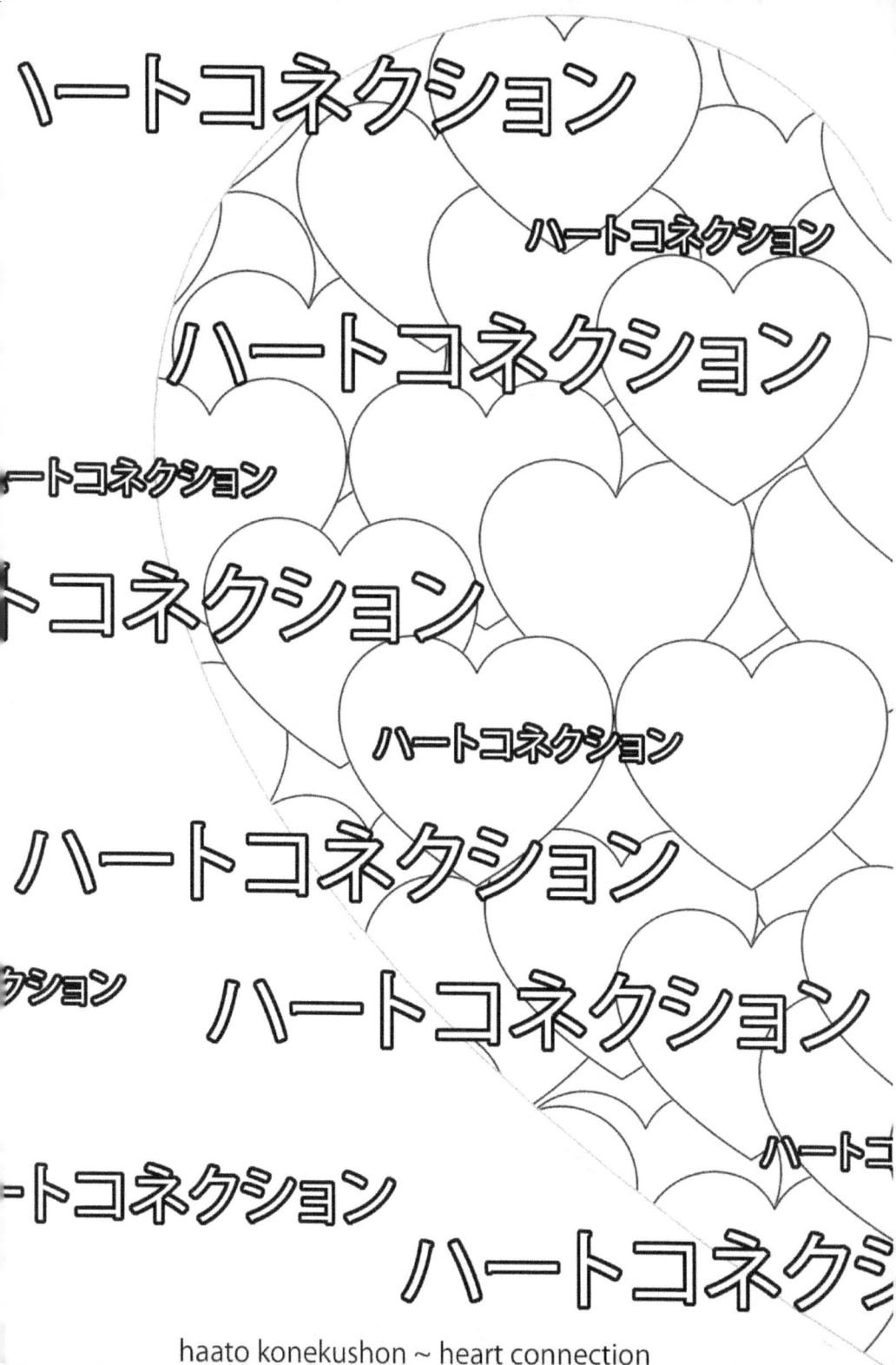

ハートコネクション

ハートコネクション

ハートコネクション

ートコネクション

トコネクション

ハートコネクション

ハートコネクション

クション

ハートコネクション

ートコネクション

ハートコ

ハートコネクシ

haato konekushon ~ heart connection

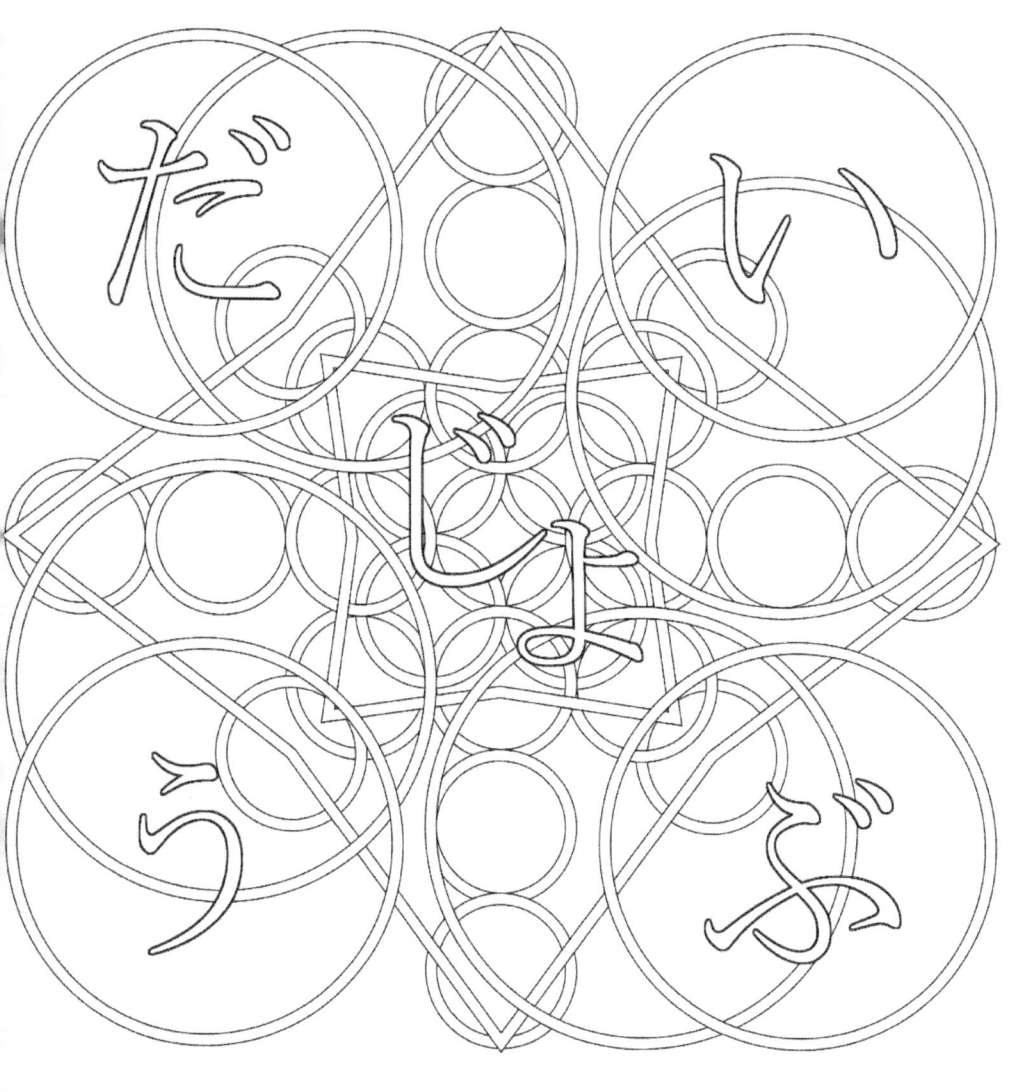

だいじょうぶ ~ daijoubu ~ it's/I'm ok

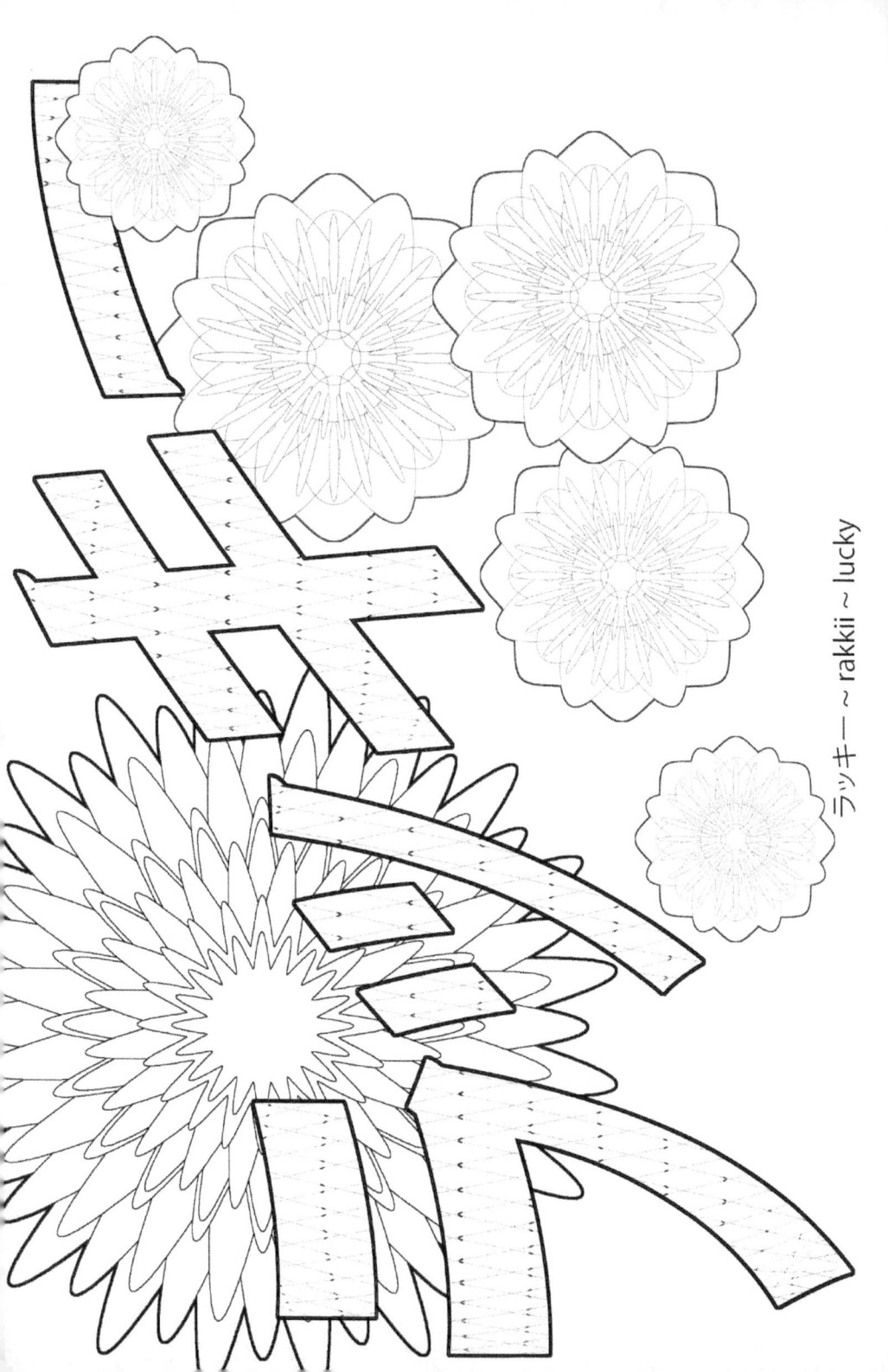

ラッキー ~ rakkii ~ lucky

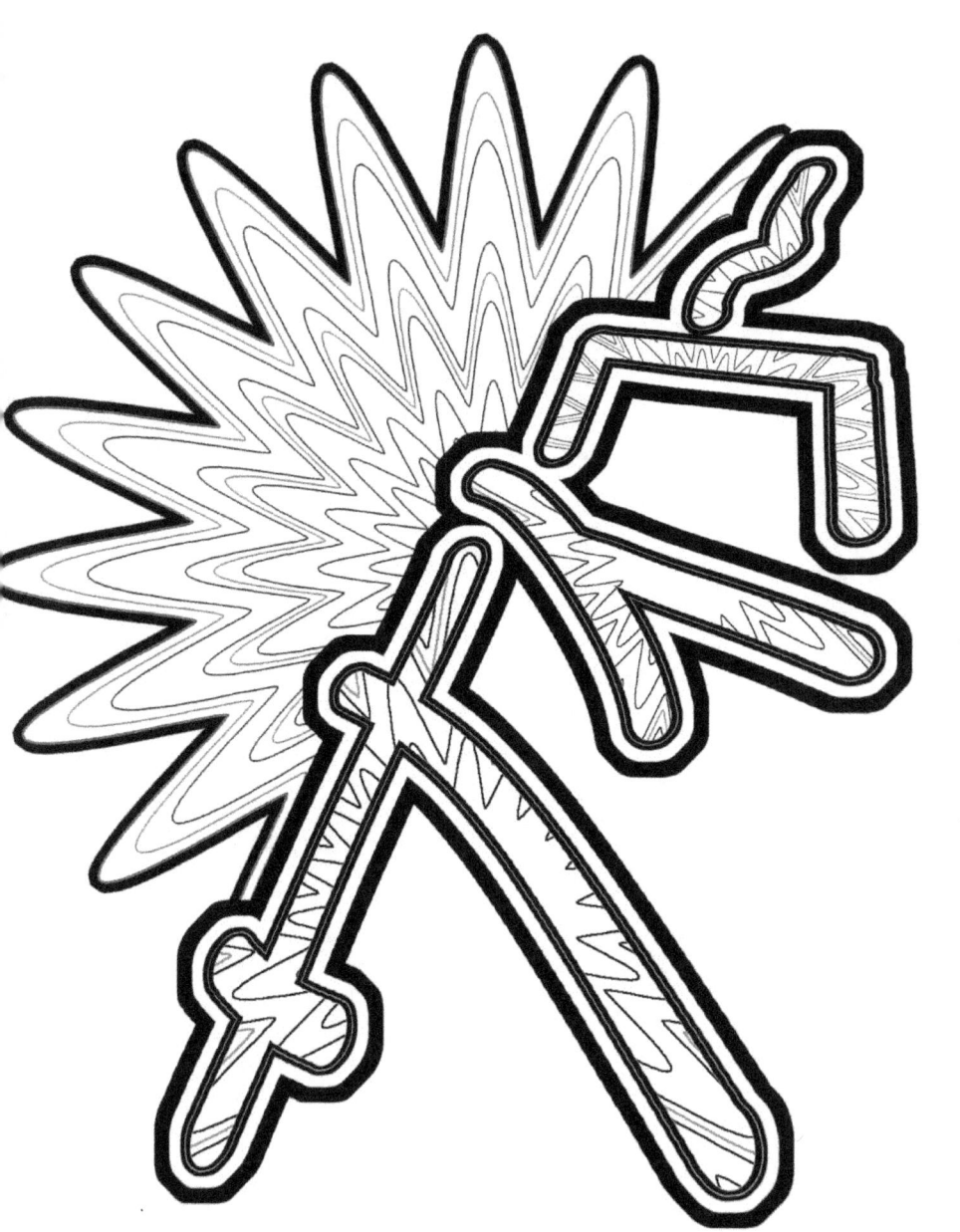

サイコー ~ saikou ~ the best

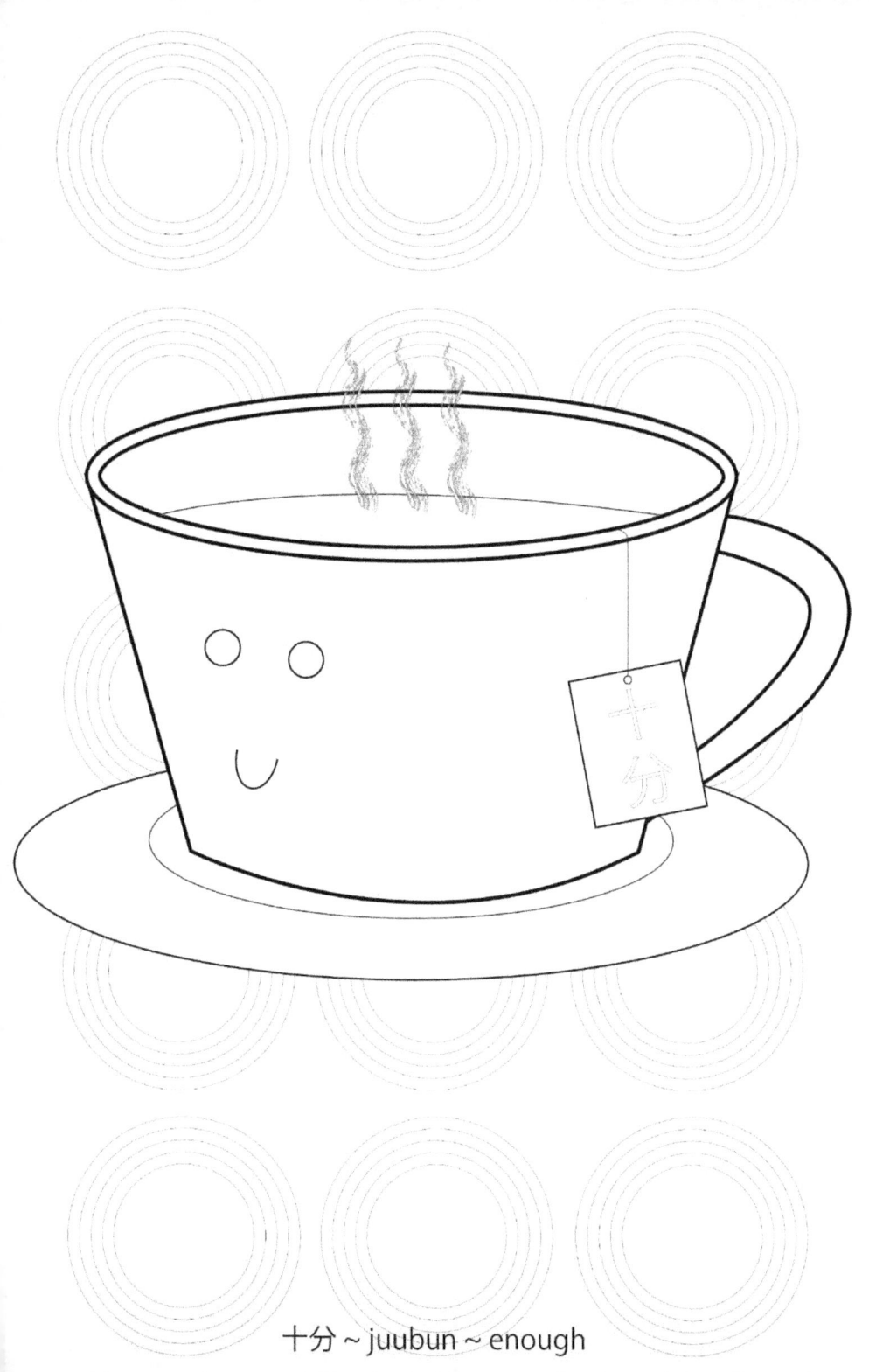

十分 ~ juubun ~ enough

暖かさ ~ atatakasa ~ warmth

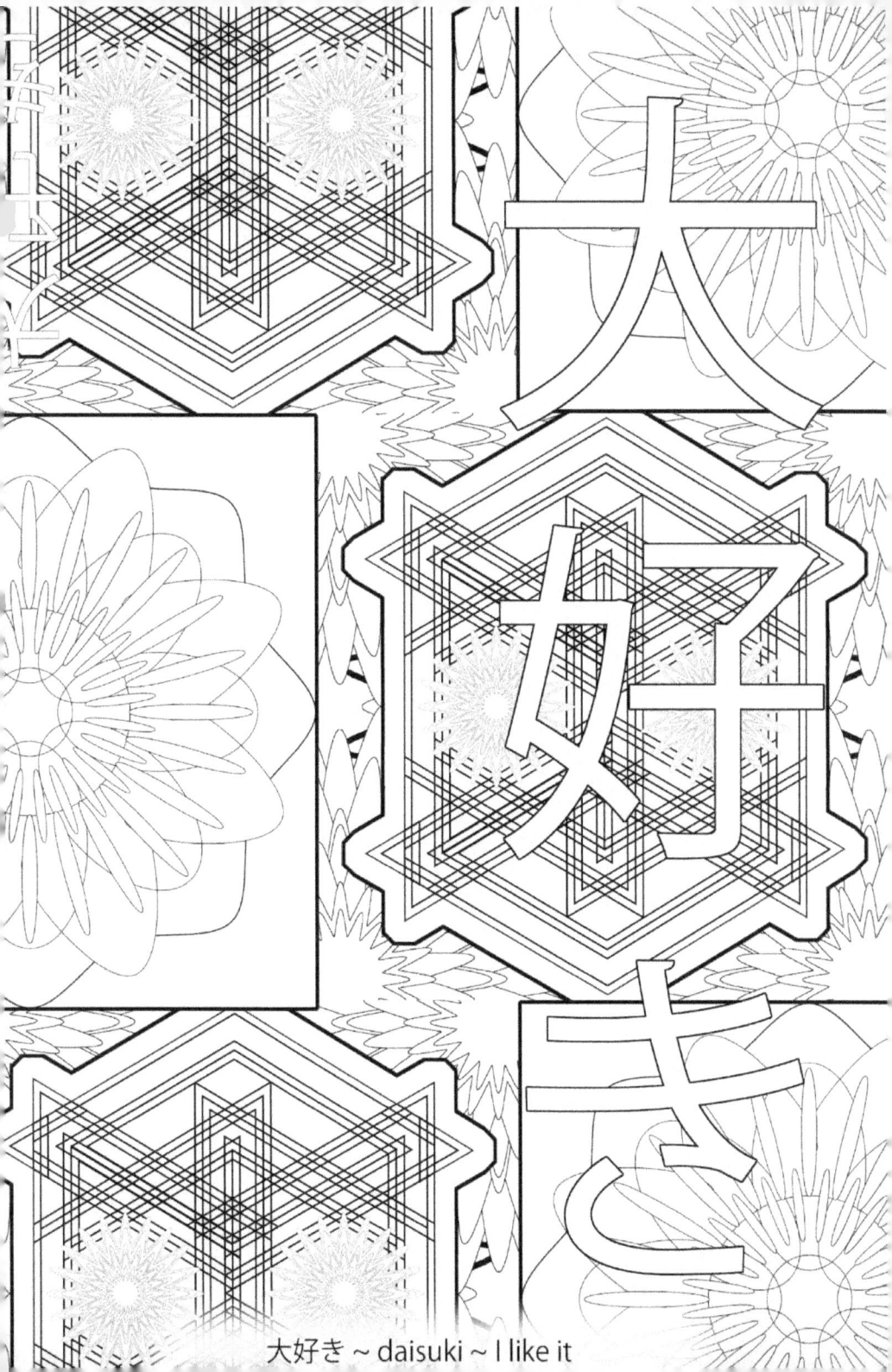

大好き ~ daisuki ~ I like it

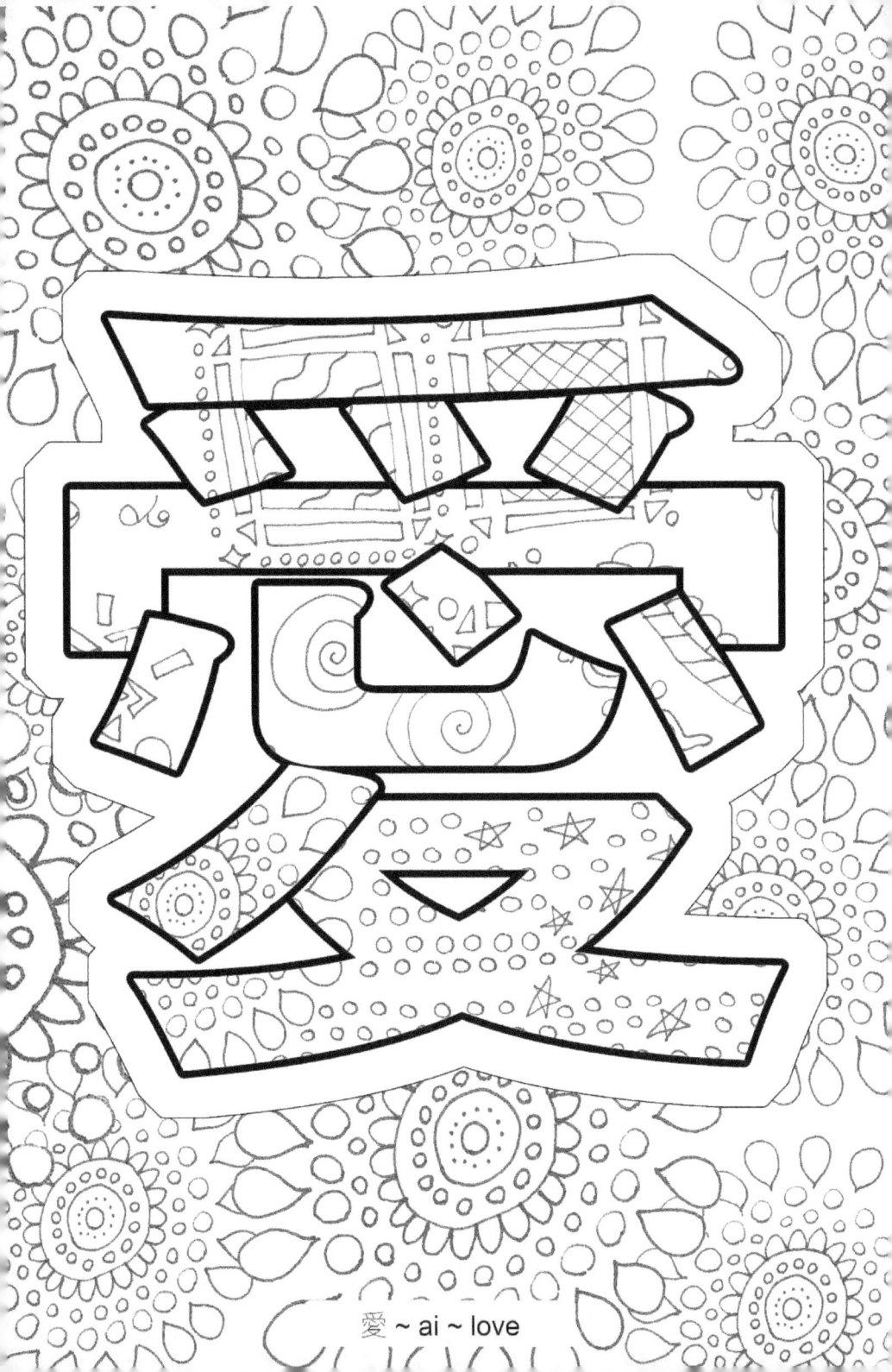

愛 ~ ai ~ love

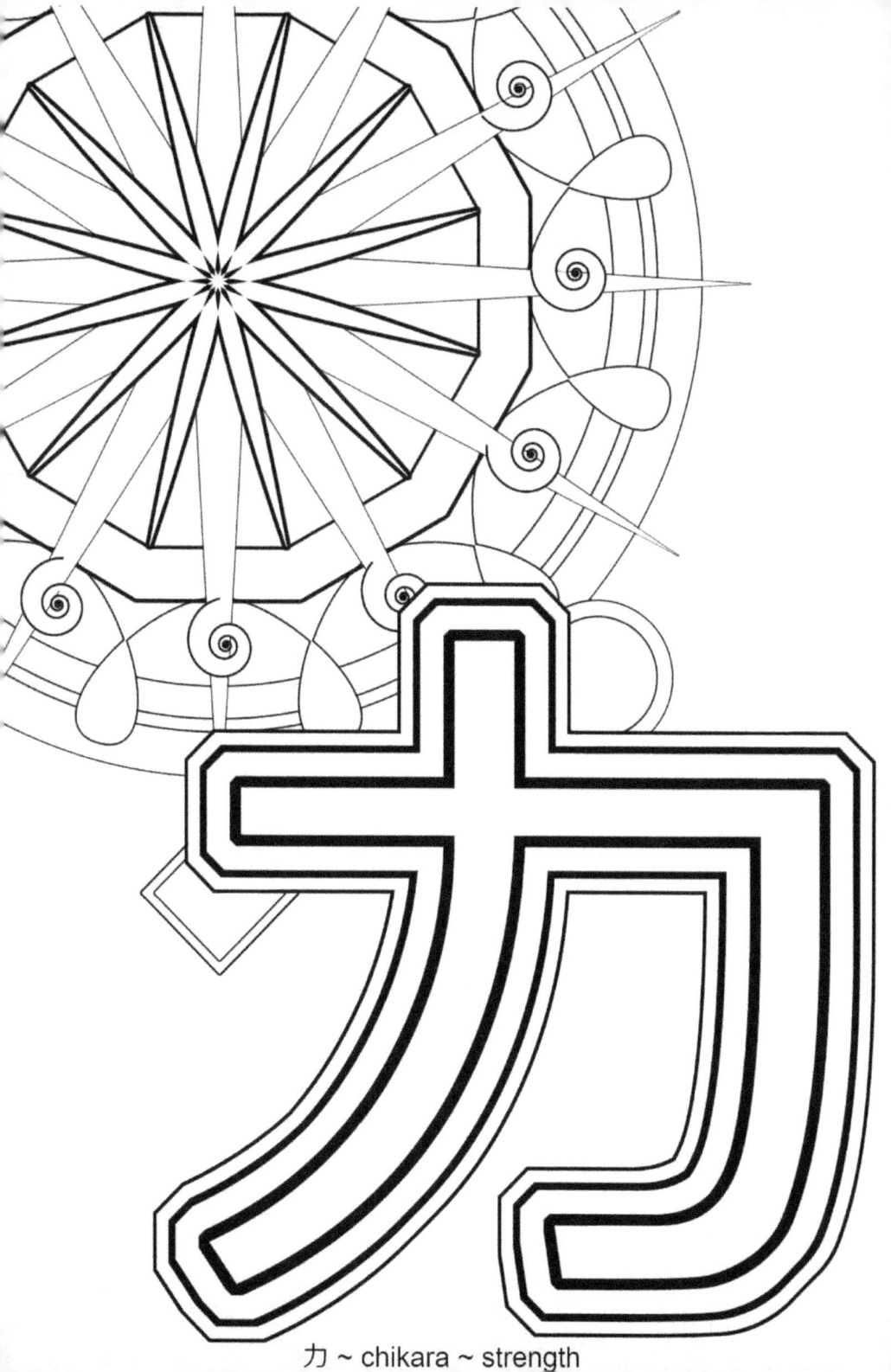

力 ~ chikara ~ strength

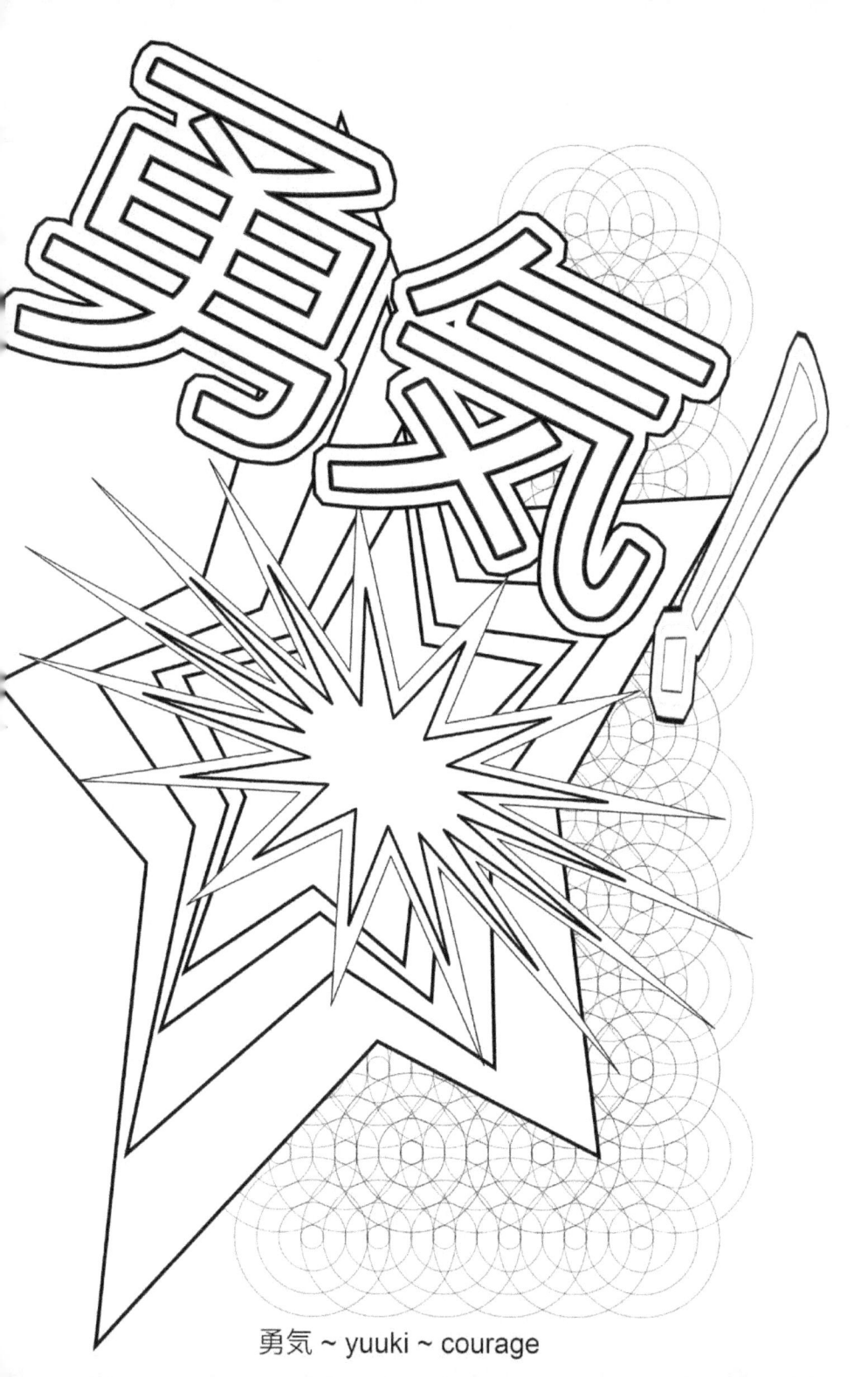

勇気 ~ yuuki ~ courage

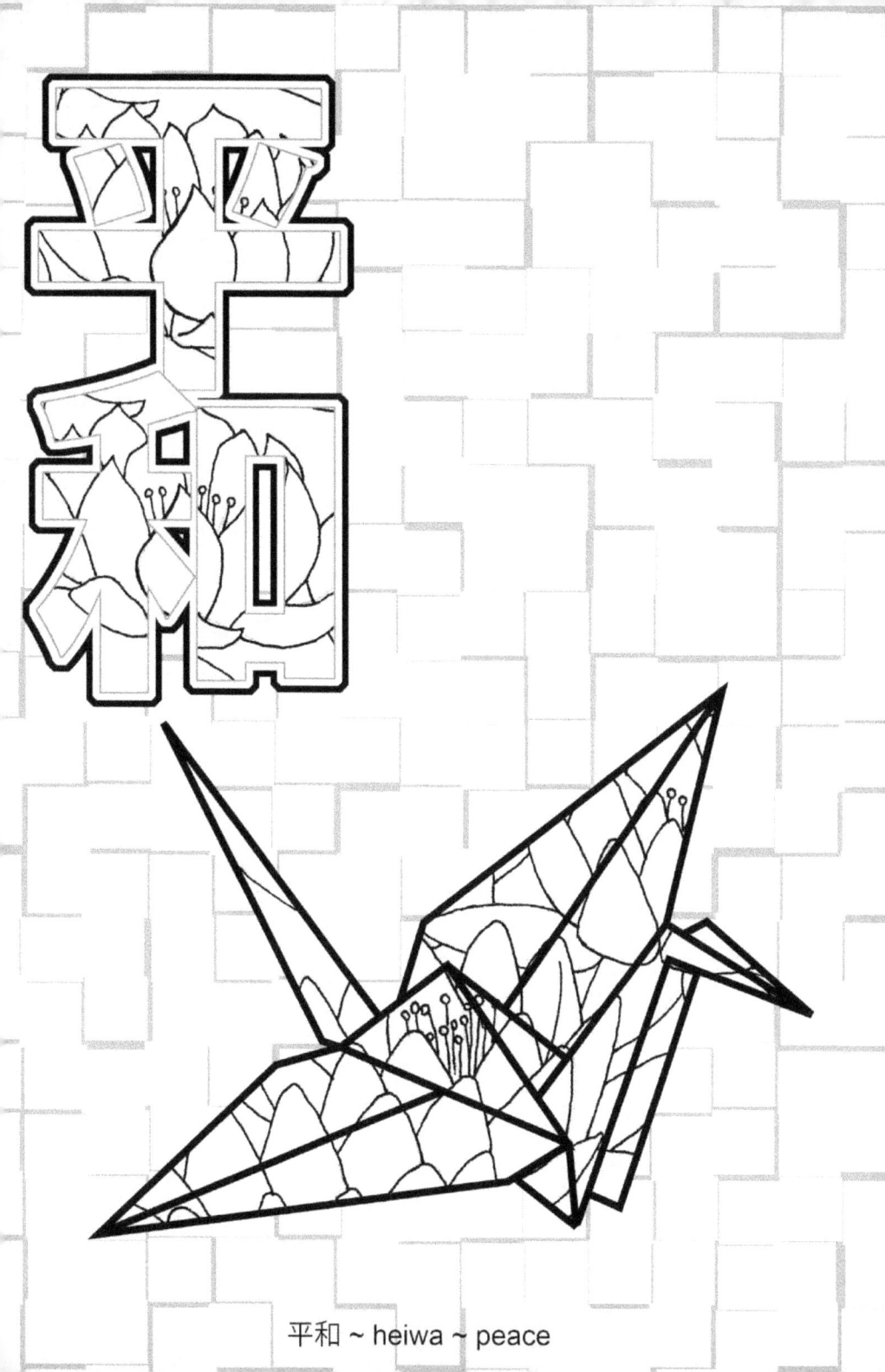

平和 ~ heiwa ~ peace

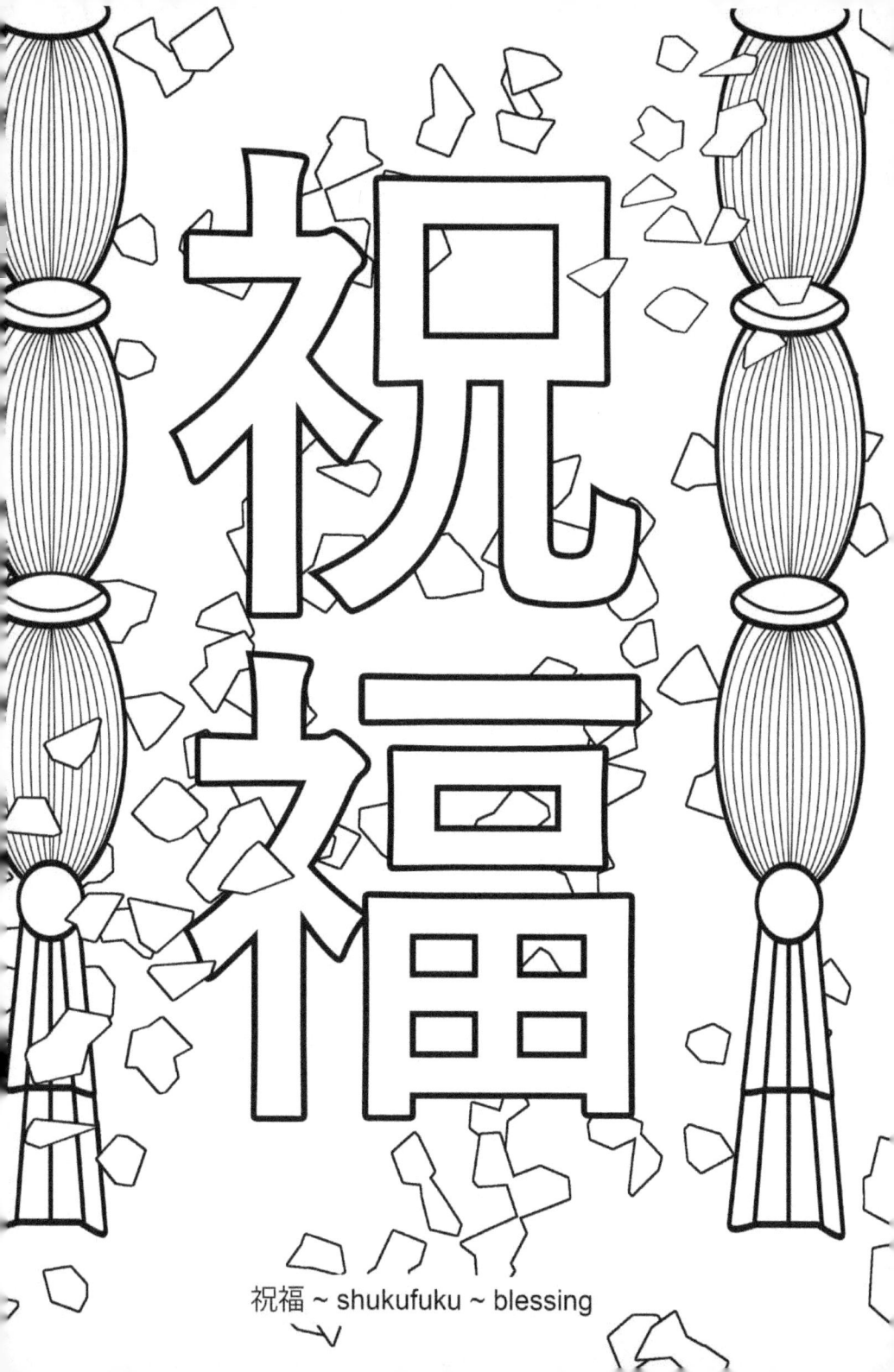

祝福 ~ shukufuku ~ blessing

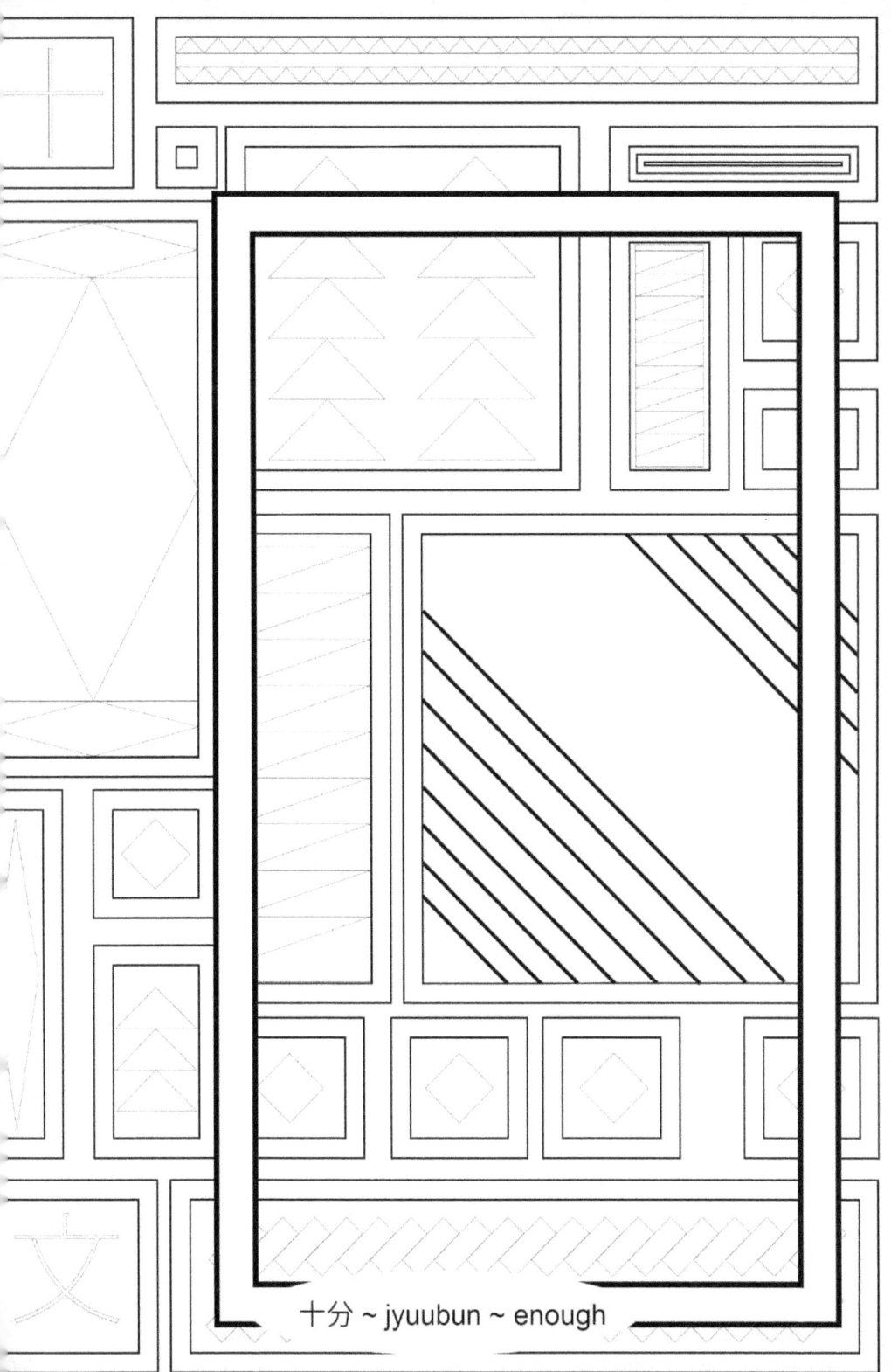

十分 ~ jyuubun ~ enough

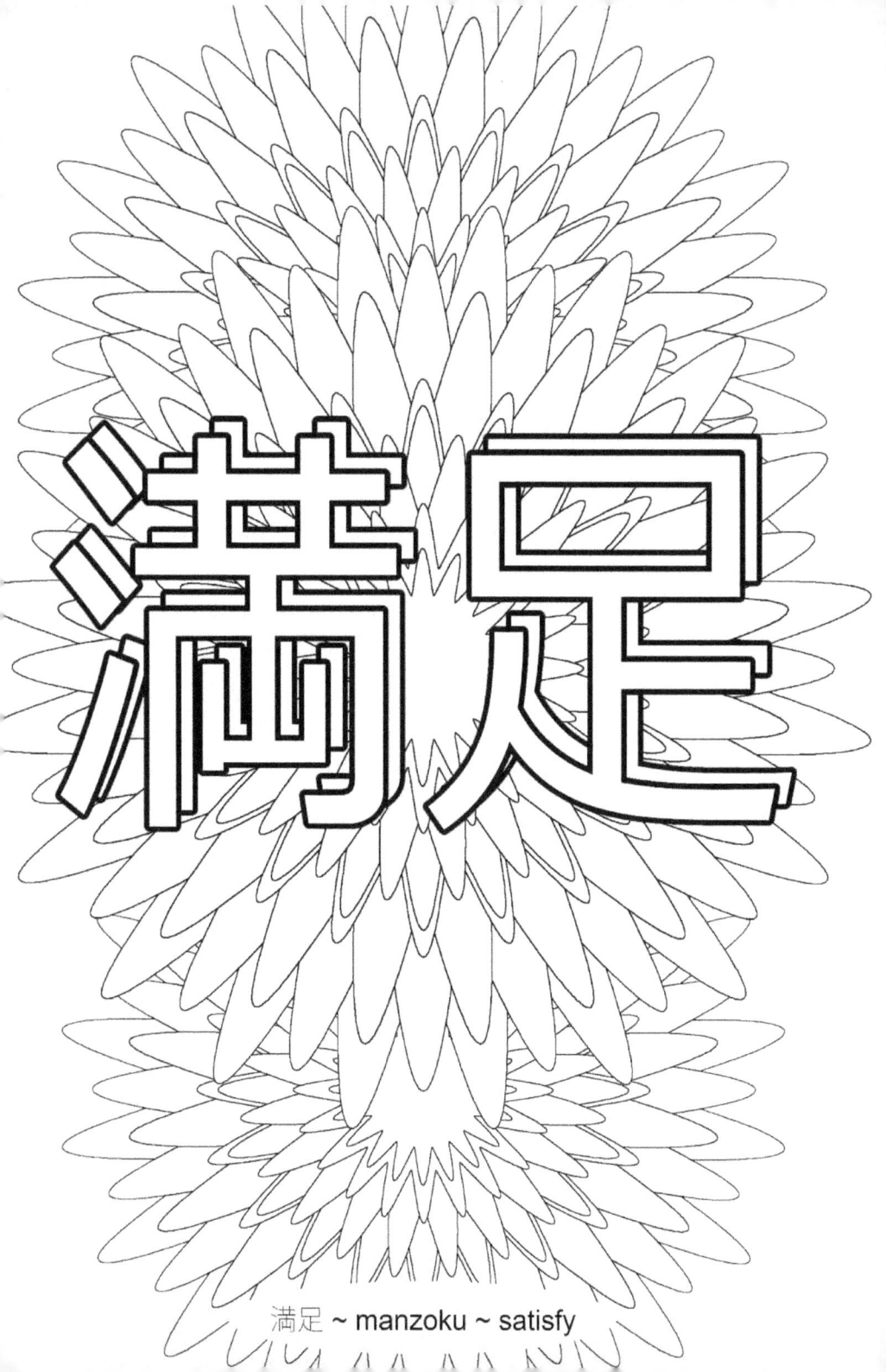

満足 ~ manzoku ~ satisfy

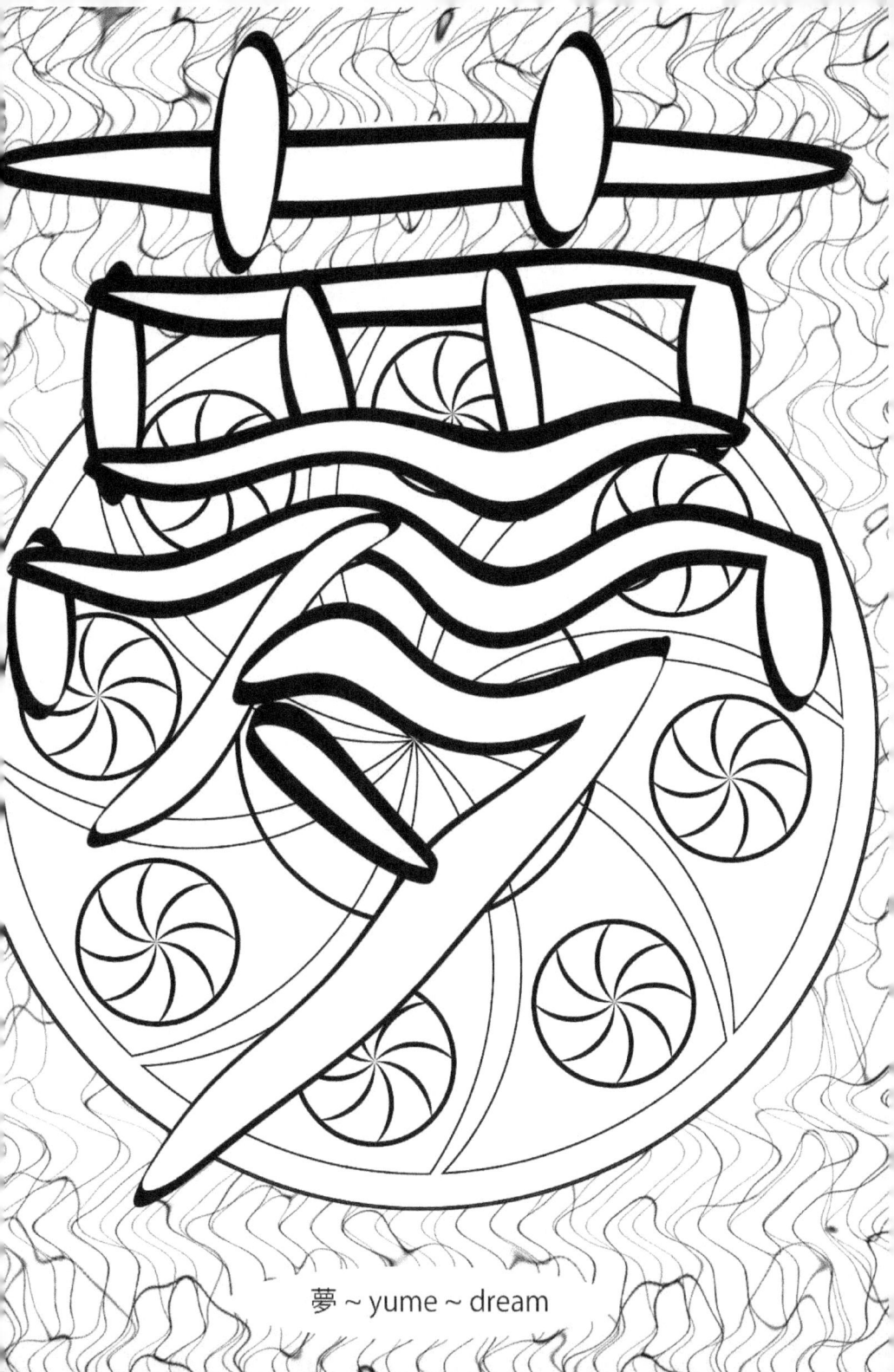

夢 ~ yume ~ dream

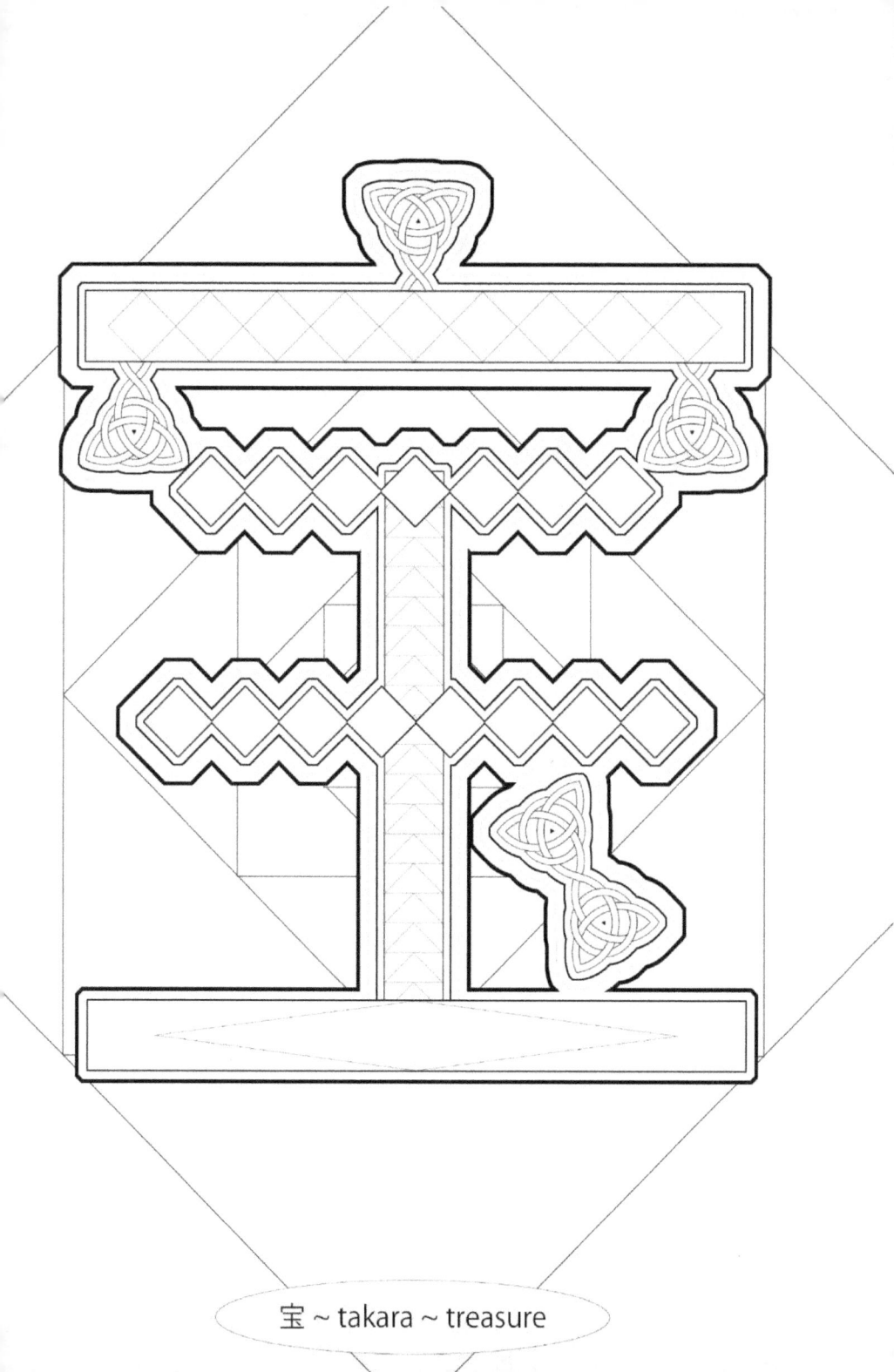

宝 ~ takara ~ treasure

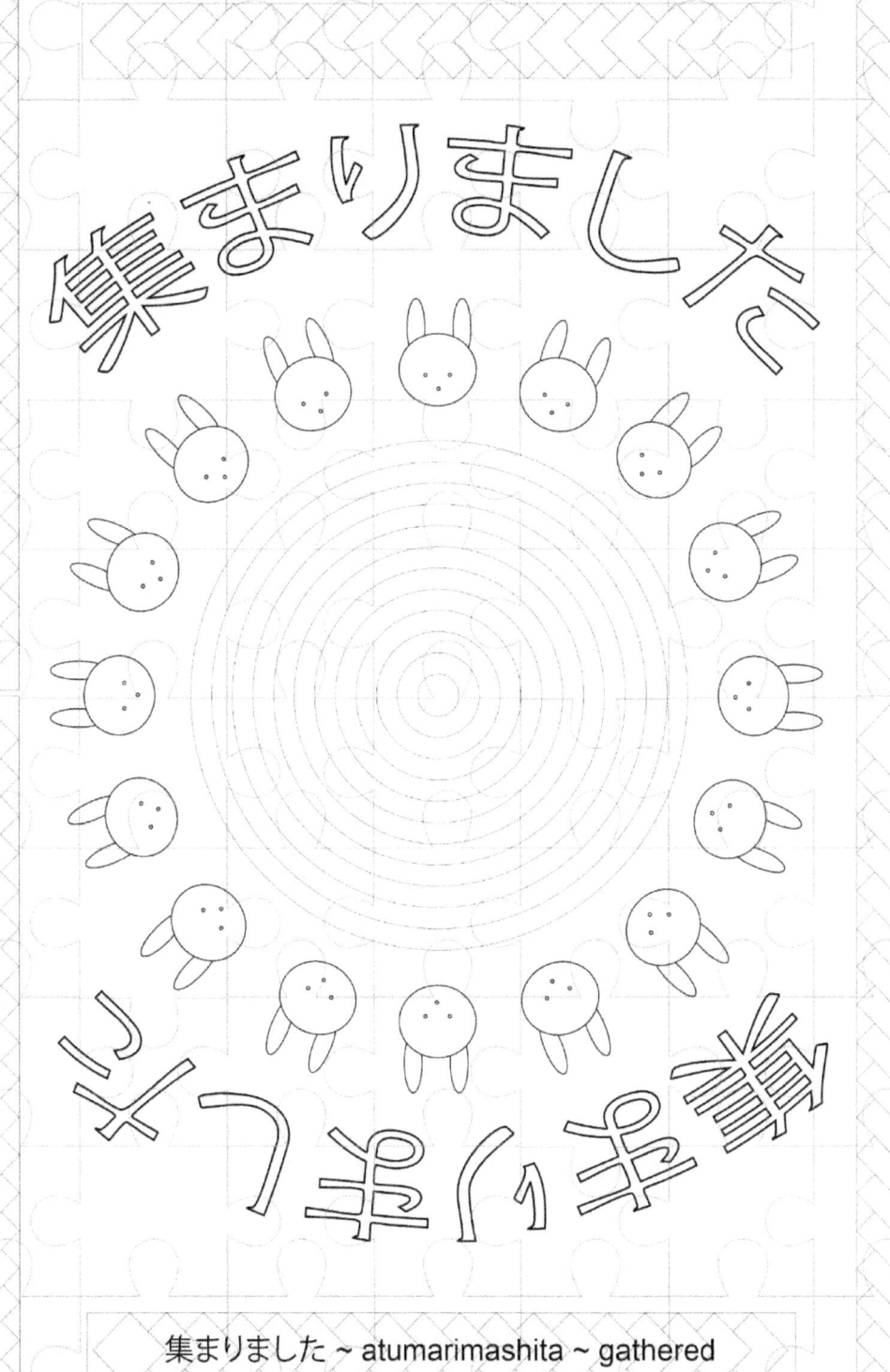

集まりました ~ atumarimashita ~ gathered

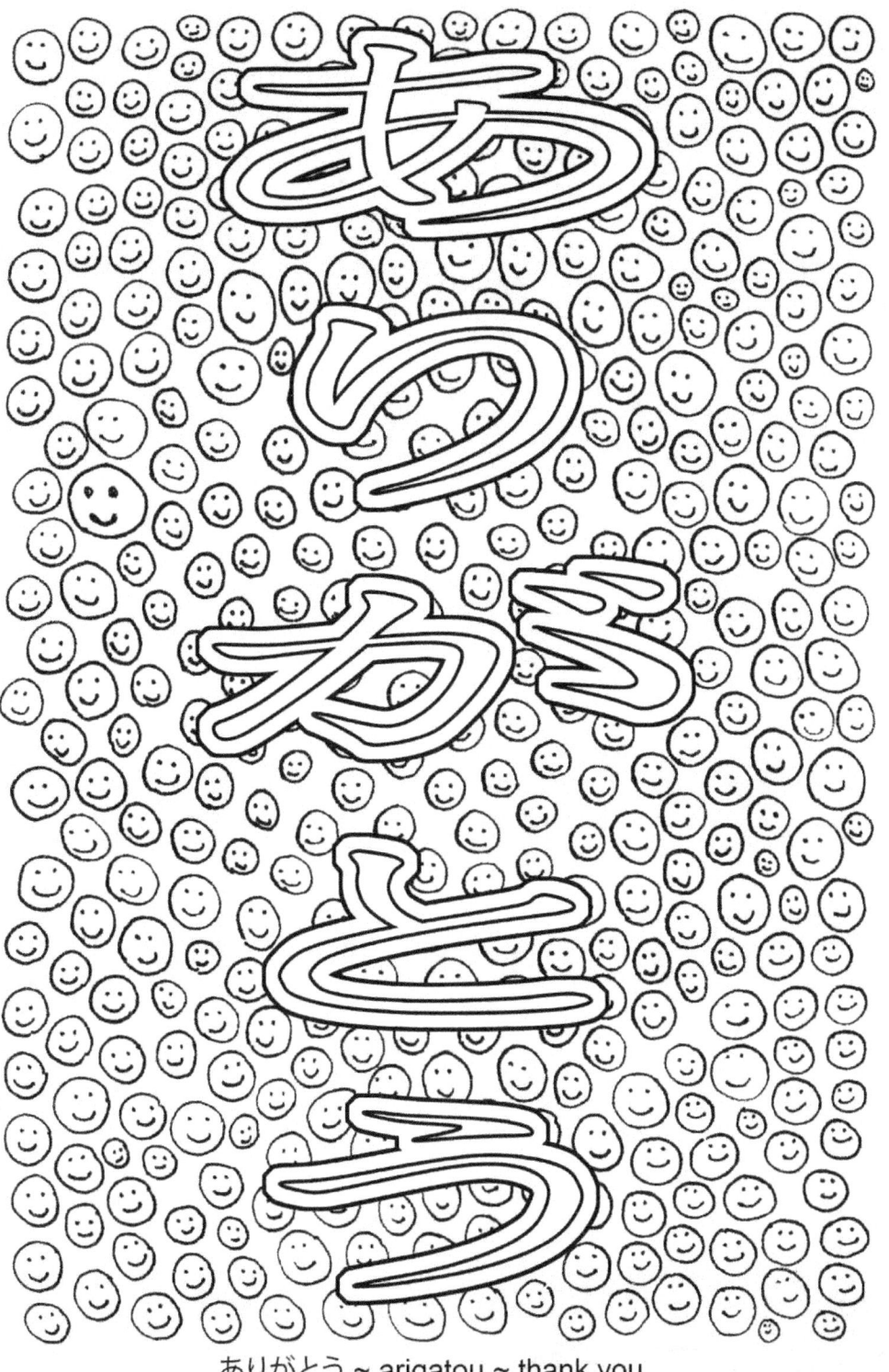

ありがとう ~ arigatou ~ thank you